little ideas
BIG RESULTS

May the favor of the Lord our God
Rest upon us;
Establish the work of our hands for us —
Yes, establish the work of our hands.

Psalm 90:17

little ideas
BIG RESULTS

Martie Byrd

Shine Like Stars

Unless otherwise identified, Scripture quotations are taken from
the Holy Bible, the New International Version.

ISBN: 978-0-578-02678-7

Dedication

In loving memory of my father, Wheeler Smith.

He would be delighted to see me
publish a book of "potty reading,"
his favorite thing to read.

He wasn't wild about salespeople, but he loved me just the same.

I love you, Pa.

Surely goodness and love will follow me
all the days of my life,
and I will dwell in the house of the Lord forever.

Psalm 23:6

Acknowledgments

There have been encouragers along the way who have cheered me on and they have made all the difference. Thanks to Barb McCandless for calling me a gifted communicator and to Creative Memories for giving me so many opportunities to speak. Thanks to Susan Childs for listening to the Lord when she was looking for a columnist and to Lauren and Joey who offer me a monthly platform to rant, share and laugh in Bella magazine. I appreciate Glynnis at P31 for my first published piece, "Confessions of a Former Know-it-All." You all took your time to edify me and I grew stronger.

For every group who has invited me to speak, I love you! You helped me grow, learn and you are a part of me. To my family who called me the "author writist", voicing my childhood dream, and seeing me that way.

To Nicole Lenderking for the fantastic photographs.

To The Gathering, for calling out my dreams.

To Angela, my exhorter. To Debi, for buying it all.

To Amy, the other part of my brain and a big part of my heart.

To Alex, Danny, Trevor, Caroline and Julia, you laugh at just the right times, listen to me read aloud, and let me sit with you at school lunch without cringing. You are my delight.

To Dave, who flirted for five hours on that U.S. Air flight all those years ago. You shared your heart and your Lord. Where would I be without you both?

And to Jesus, You are my All in All. You know.

Easter Morning
Roanoke, VA

Table of Contents

Introduction
10 Second Tidy

Section 1: Sales
Would you like fries with that?
The Debi Decision
Everyone wants to buy
People come crabby…and that's okay!
No is just a word
Conquering Phone Phobia
Snob Appeal

Section 2: Dreams and Goals
Dreams with a Deadline
The Laundry Lesson
But I don't feel like it
No Excuses
Reward yourself
Shampoo, Rinse, Repeat

Section 3: Leadership
My MBA
How to be a Good Leader
Team building for wimps
Just Keep Swimmin'!
Run to the problem
The Theme Team

Section 4: What's it all about?
Take a chance
How to make my Lord your Lord
Confessions of a former know-it-all
It's not about me
Who am I in Christ?

10 Second Tidy

I am a slightly crazed mother of many. I used to want things perfect. Now I just want things done. Can you relate? My poor husband! When we were first married, I insisted that we get up and do chores every Saturday morning. That's what I did growing up and that was the way I knew how to do it. Dave was a good sport and we lived in a tidy house...until we started adding kids to it. Kids may be little, but they make a big mess! Lots of kids...even bigger mess!

So I've learned how to make every minute count. I no longer have time to do things perfectly. Life is too short for perfect! I've learned that it's enough to just get the thing done. I've tried to pass this principle on to the kids. For instance, when they were little, I taught them how to pick up the family room in a hurry. I'd announce "10 Second Tidy!" and everyone would spring into action. We'd quickly throw the toys in the bin, gather the laundry in a pile, and flush the toilet. Voila! A moderately clean house...in less than a minute.

This is my fast pick up book on Sales and Marketing. You picked it up because you want to learn and apply a few new principles which will greatly increase your success. You can take ten seconds or so and read just one idea. You have time to do that. Life and laundry dictates that you don't have a ton of time to invest in yourself. Maybe one day you'll go for an MBA, or heck, even just take a course online. But today's probably not that day. That doesn't mean you can't succeed in a big way!

Make today your day to learn one new thing. Just one little thing. Little idea, big result. That is, if you apply it! So that's the task. Learn one thing and apply it. I've worked with a lot of women. I know many of us don't want to try something new until we think we can do it perfectly. We don't want to set a goal unless we're sure we can meet it. We don't want to start a team until we feel qualified to be a leader. We're going to have to snap out of that thinking. Take a little idea, do it and you'll see a big result. Ready, set, go! You won't get anywhere by sitting still.

I know you are busy. That's why each section is a quick read. Each idea is very do-able, no matter what else is going on in your life. You'll find that as you blend each idea into your life, it becomes second nature. Then you're ready for the next idea. Each quick lesson is something you can do, or overcome, or think about. Read a chapter, and think about it. Apply what you've learned. Take a minute…heck, take a few seconds, and do those things.

Scripture tells us that there's a time for everything. There's a season for every activity. Yet the world teaches us we need to balance things. Balance is a myth. Balance implies there are only two things. For instance, you balance your kids and your business. You stand in the middle with just those two things, trying to balance them, like an old-fashioned scale. That's just not how it is.

In truth, we have many more than two priorities. We want to be good wives and mothers. We want to be women of faith and be involved in our faith communities. We want to be friends, sisters, encouragers. We also want to live in a comfortable, sane home. We'd like to drive the car pool, volunteer at the library, even occasionally take a hot bath. In short, we want to do well, and make our lives count. That's going to require a lot more than balance.

Instead, this book is about blending. Our lives are like a cup of yogurt with the fruit on the bottom. We need to learn how to blend all the elements of life together so that each bite of life is satisfying and flavorful! It can be done! I've done it and I know many other women who are doing it, too. They are making happy homes and successful businesses while volunteering, praying and caring for their community. You can, too!

When I started in direct sales, my sponsor told me to keep the company's consultant guide in the bathroom. I thought she was kidding me!

"Just pick it up and read a page or two a day," she counseled.

It turned out to be good advice. I read that book over and over just because it was available and well, I had the time. My father called that type of a book "potty reading." He was famous for sending clippings and short articles for that very purpose. This is my potty reading book on sales. It's full of little ideas that will yield big results!

There is a time for everything and a season for every activity under heaven.
Ecclesiastes 3:1

little ideas about

sales

Whatever you do,
do it all for the
Glory of God.

1 Corinthians 10:31

Would you like fries with that?

I always wanted to work at McDonald's. Naturally, when I was sixteen, it was the first place I applied. I got the job! I was ecstatic! Free Filet-o-Fish and french fries. Cute boys working on the grill. A paycheck! It was my first job and it was my introduction to sales.

Now, McDonald's is not a high-pressure sales environment. After all, people come in to the restaurant intending to eat. They are hungry and thirsty. In general they order what they want to have. Long ago, before Value Meals were invented, our manager explained to us how we could increase each and every sale, simply by asking a question. We were trained to end each sale by suggesting an add-on item. "Would you like fries with that?" If they had ordered fries, the question was, "Would you like large fries?" If they ordered a small drink, we'd ask if they wanted to supersize it. It didn't feel like pressure, it felt like friendship. After all, who wants salty fries without a drink? Who wants to get in their car and realize they forgot to order the apple pie they wanted? If I offered fries and the customer said no, that didn't hurt my feelings. I didn't invent McDonald's! I wasn't actually making the food. I would get paid whether I sold small Cokes or large Cokes. This was a safe and fun introduction to sales.

When I got out of college, my career was in advertising and marketing. You'll laugh, but in many ways it wasn't that different from McDonald's. Clients would come in and need a solution. They had a product or service they wanted to promote. The copywriters and art directors would ask questions to further define their wants and needs. Then, once the campaign was conceived, we would suggest add-ons. If they requested a radio commercial, we showed them how it would be more effective if we tied that concept in with clever billboards around town. It worked!

When my children were tiny, I wanted a little job out of the house so I started working at Gap Kids. It was delightful sharing my mom-spertise (expertise of a mom) with the expecting and new parents. In particular, I remember a sales competition. Whoever sold the most jeans would get a prize. I wanted the prize, but I also wanted to help find solutions for the customers. I had already seen how very difficult it was for parents and kids to find jeans that they both agreed on. I learned it was well-worth the time to ask questions and offer solutions. The husky boys needed elastic waist jeans. The wispy girls needed adjustable waist jeans. After spending twenty or thirty minutes with a customer, we identified the perfect jeans for their child. At that point, I simply suggested, "You should buy two pairs so you don't have to go through this again for a while!" 9 out of 10 moms agreed that would was very wise. Many thanked me profusely for the suggestion. I won the competition and it was so easy. All I did, really, was suggestive selling, just like I did at McDonald's. It was just another version of "Would you like fries with that?"

But here's where the real magic occurred. I saw the appreciation in both the eyes of the kids (particularly the pre-teens!) and the moms. They were so grateful. So sincerely grateful that I asked! They thought it was such a great idea! I realized that by caring, asking, listening and suggesting solutions, I happened to be selling. Selling a lot. Selling well. I loved it!

Next, I started my own business with a direct marketing company. You would imagine that if I could sell french fries and jeans, I would be able to sell a product I loved and valued. It was a product I had used for several years. It had brought value to my life. I wanted to share it with friends, old and new. But I was afraid. Why? I was now in a situation where I would profit from my sales. That froze me in my tracks. I was afraid that potential profit would make me insincere. How silly! I am the same person whether people buy from me or not!

Besides, we are providing a service. We should make a profit! Guys, if it is costing you money to represent your product, something is wrong. Profit is good. Money is fine. It's simply a tool. As long as we don't value the money above the people, we are in good shape.

From a 16-year old kid to a thirty-something year old small business owner, I had to evolve. I had to become okay with success and with making a profit. Perhaps there is something keeping you frozen in the same place in your business. Today is the day for you to thaw out! Ask yourself these questions:

- *Do I believe in my product?*
- *Do I see how it positively impacts lives?*
- *Do I deserve to succeed?*
- *Is it okay to make a profit?*
- *Why am I in this business?*

Find your true passion in what you do, then share, share, share! You are adding value to lives all around you…believe it!

The Debi Decision

"I want it all. I want it now. I want it organized for me."

So said Debi. She sat quietly through my presentation and seemed very impatient. She didn't meet my eyes or ask questions, leading me to believe she wasn't interested. Boy, was I wrong.

"I want it all. I want it now. I want it organized for me." I didn't even know how to sell the whole kit-n-caboodle! Up until that point in my business, I was selling piecemeal. One item to one person, another item to another. I hadn't packaged things in kits. I was happy to make a $5 sale, and here was someone who wanted to buy the store. Her initial purchase was over $300. Her purchase exceeded the total amount I had sold in my first few months of business.

Needless to say, I learned a lot from Debi. We became good friends and she often described how she felt at that first presentation. She shared:

- You had me at hello. I was interested from the first moment I saw your products.

- You assume the negative with lines like "You don't have to get anything tonight." This is bad!

- Instead, offer the positive, "You can walk out of here with everything you want tonight."

- Don't make people wait when their decisions are made. Let them buy!

Could she be right? I was flabbergasted! Why was I assuming the negative? Debi made me think. After I examined my heart, I could see how I was speaking from a position of fear and insecurity. I didn't yet wholly believe in my product and the advantages of it. I needed to really search my heart. Why was I representing a product I didn't believe in? I did believe in it! I did! But I didn't want to be turned down. I had a deep fear of rejection. And I did want to be liked. We all do.

Maybe you can relate. Maybe some of these same issues are tormenting you. I remember that day like it was yesterday. I had some issues to work through. It came down to this. I didn't want to talk anyone into anything, I didn't want anyone to feel pressured, and I didn't want to, in short, "sell."

Sell was a four-letter word in my home growing up. My father was skeptical and felt that every salesperson was a shyster (one who is professionally unscrupulous.) As you can imagine, that fear was communicated to the children. I had a subconscious fear of selling! Or being sold! For instance, if a salesperson approached us at a department store, we always had the same answer, "Just looking." That was the only way we knew to keep the salesperson from influencing our purchasing decisions. By sending them away! Of course, this meant we never received the helpful suggestions a salesperson can offer. There had to be a better way!

How did I reconcile my fear of sales with wanting to help people? I had to learn that selling people what they want and can use is a service. It's a delight to help others find solutions! My fears gave me a false perspective. Debi helped by showing me the value of my product. In one presentation she valued my product more than I did after three years of using it. She helped open my eyes to see my product through her eyes. She was new to the product but saw the intrinsic value. It met a need in her life. It was something she had been looking for. She was sold …in a good way!

Until that presentation, I didn't really believe in my product. I knew it was great for me and my family, but I didn't understand that others would appreciate it, too. I was afraid of forcing something on them, so I provided excuses of why they didn't need to buy. By saying things like, "You can start small" or "You don't need to buy anything tonight" or "It's okay if you want to look around", I was doing nothing but confusing my potential customers. Did I believe in my product? Or didn't I?

Yes! Debi helped me to see what I was doing through fresh eyes. It was an invaluable service. Ask a good friend to come along as you do your workshops or presentations. Be open and receptive to what her observations are. Be willing to hear what she says and be willing to change. We all can tweak what we do in order to be better at it. Good can be made better; better can be made best. Unless you think you are already the absolute best at what you do, you have room for improvement!

Thanks, Debi!

Everyone wants to buy...

But no one wants to get sold. What's the difference? When someone is buying, it is their choice. When someone is being sold, it's more about the salesperson than the purchaser. How can you make your offers about them buying and not you selling?

Always remember what attracted you to your product. Never, ever forget what it was like the first time you saw it. What did you like? What were your concerns? What questions did you need to have answered? Be frank and honest about your own experiences.

Let it be about them. Let your prospective customers put their hands on the merchandise. Let them try it on, experiment with the items, discuss the product among themselves. They are far more likely to listen to one another than they are likely to listen to you. Why? Because they know you are the salesperson and they don't want to be sold.

Make it easy to buy. Streamline the decision-making process. Yes, you may have a bag full of tricks and a catalog full of hundreds of items. This is all very overwhelming to people who are just being introduced to the line that you carry. Proceed with simplicity. Organize items in starter kits. Offer special groupings of the most popular things. Have the order forms filled out and ready to go.

Be calm and cheerful. You come with a sales goal and an expectation for the presentation. These goals will key you up and once again, make it more about you and your goals than them and their needs. Pray about the show on the way over, but leave your expectations at the door. Make your expectation that you will have a fun time and meet some new friends and hopefully match your products to their needs. Period.

Don't measure success by how much cash you carry away. Success is in the long-term, not in the short-term. There have been many times that I have left a show feeling disappointed because I didn't sell a lot of merchandise. Then I'm wowed when those customers become big purchasers or team members down the road. Success does not have to do with a full money bag. It has to do with feeling good about yourself, your product and your time. The sales will come.

Listen more than you speak. The Bible tells us to be quick to listen and slow to speak. This is hard when you have a lot of enthusiasm about your product and you feel that you have a captive audience. Keep your presentation short, simple and tailored to their needs. It's not about your need to impart every bit of information about your product. Encourage questions. Again, participants are far more likely to listen to each other than to you. Get the conversation ball rolling and be open to questions! Be willing to leave your agenda behind. Listen more than you speak.

Keep the purchasing time private. It's a great idea to step a few feet away from the group in order to do your sales slips in private. One, you'll be less flustered than you may be in a room full of chatting women! Two, it's a much more comfortable atmosphere for your prospective customer to get her questions answered and for you to review her order form. Not every woman wants her friends to see what she is buying or how much she is spending. Sitting apart during this portion of the evening will also allow you a better chance to get to know the participant, one on one.

Answer questions but don't get desperate. Because of our goals, we sometimes pressure the purchaser. We start putting on the big squeeze. Resist the temptation to do this. After all, you don't like to be pressured, why would she? Instead, let your prospective customer tell you what she needs in order to make her decision. Say things like, "How can I help you make your decision tonight?" or "Do you need any more information?"

Let her come to you. Everyone wants to buy but no one wants to be sold. Your gracious attitude will pay back tenfold. After all, if you earn a pressured sale, you may have the sale but you will also gain a reputation as being high pressure. Word will get out. This will not help you in the long run.

Laugh! Be a carrier of joy at your event. Be willing to join in the silliness of a group of friends together. If there's a time, tell a funny story but keep it short and relevant. We all deal with more than enough heaviness in our lives. Be a light!

Be purposeful with your time. Respect your own time and the time allotted for the event by carefully planning out the evening. I cringe whenever team members talk about their shows lasting into the wee hours. That is never a good way to book additional shows. Instead, say something like, "I'm going to share about the products for a few minutes, then we'll talk about the products together for about ten minutes. After that, I'll be in the kitchen to answer your questions and help you make your choices. Amy has some great desserts for us to try!" Women tend to tune out and mentally start doing their grocery list if they think they will be trapped in a long presentation. Keep it short and lively.

Don't rush out. The time after the purchasing is the time that friendships are formed and solidified. If you rush out as soon as the last participant has ordered, you are missing this golden opportunity. Often the people who linger are the ones who are interested in the business and want to get to know you better. Don't rush home. Enjoy the end of the evening as much as the beginning.

People come crabby...and that's okay!

Once I got over my fear of talking to one or two people, I was ready to speak to a group. What I learned is that each group has one or two people who really seem to "get" me. They make eye contact, laugh at my jokes, and nod when I'm talking. These are all signs of affirmation that I need and want. (Alternately, there are always people who do the opposite. They may look down or away, read brochures while I'm talking, fold their arms, or scowl. This unnerves and distracts me horribly.)

It's important that you focus on those who are smiling! Their non-verbal cues are encouraging. They will literally give you more confidence and more courage. Do not focus on the scowlers. If you do, you will feel your confidence draining out of your pedicured toes. I have met many women who stop conducting shows simply because of the scowlers. That's just not right! Here's the great news...there is always a mix! The key is to find the smilers and direct your attention to them. (Not ignore the others! Of course not. But focus on the ones who are inspiring you in return.)

Imagine you are speaking to a group of friends. This is how they will break out into segments.

- 33%: *I'm interested!*

- 33%: *My friend made me come but I might be persuaded to be interested.*

- 33%: *I had a terrible day and there is absolutely nothing you can say or do to make me interested.*

People-pleasing consultants will tend to stumble when presented with the bad-moodies. We react in one of two ways. Either we bend over backwards to try to appeal to them or we get freaked out and freeze for the whole group. You don't need to do either of these things. Sure, there are some people who may not be interested today. That's okay. Repeat these words, "It's not about me. It's not about me."

People come in bad moods. The reasons don't have anything to do with you or your product. For instance, they may be concerned about a suspicious mole they just found, worried about their 16-year-old son who is starting to drive, or mentally rehashing an argument with their husband. You can't know what's going on, and you don't have to know. It's enough that they got a night out. Treat them with respect and cheer, but don't feel it's your job to persuade, cajole or sell them. Today's not the day. And that's okay!

I always arrive early in order to find my smiling faces. Every single conversation outside of the presentation is solid gold. No one has their defenses up, no one is afraid they're being sold. Be there early to help your hostess and strike up some conversations. I always start with, "How do you know Karen?" Listen more than you speak! These conversations help you understand who is in your audience, what they are about, and what challenges they face. I love to meet people anyway, and the examples we use in our presentation are much more powerful if they reference the people in the room.

Of course, every conversation is different. The very best way to learn is to accompany a senior consultant as she goes about her business. Watch and learn! But as an example, I've scripted what would be a typical conversation for me as people are arriving before a presentation. Here it goes:

> "Hi, I'm Martie. How do you know Karen?"
>
> "Our kids go to preschool together."
>
> "Awesome! Tell me about your kids."

"I have three, ages 6, 4 and 2."

"Boys? Girls? Or a combo pack?"

"Two boys and a girl."

"What a beautiful family. You are on the go, I bet."

"I am! That's why I look so exhausted!"

"You look awesome! Tonight is about you, so relax! Karen has some lemonade, can I get you a glass?"

Be gracious and caring. Even if it's not your house, answer the door and help the hostess in any way you can. Be welcoming and interested. You will find that when you do this, you'll have many smiling faces in your audience by the time you begin your presentation. You might even help turn someone's frown upside down!

No is just a word

We just don't like the word "no." We're not comfortable saying it. We're not comfortable hearing it. Maybe it's because as moms, we train toddlers to stop saying it every ten seconds! We don't like to hear "no." What's the deal? It's just a word, isn't it? I once heard a phenomenally successful consultant summarize business like this:

"Some will. Some won't. So what? Someone's waiting."

It helped me put the word "no" in perspective. I sometimes say no and I certainly hope that you say no once in a while. It's okay. It doesn't mean we should stop asking! When we say no to an opportunity, it's a personal decision. But it's not one that should be taken personally! No can mean:

- *Not at this time.*
- *It's not a right fit for me.*
- *I don't understand what you are asking.*
- *I need to know more.*

It does not mean, as many tender-hearted women think, that:

- *I am not liked!*
- *I have been rejected!*
- *I was wrong to ask!*
- *I should never (ever, ever, ever!) ask anyone again.*

I'm not kidding. I have felt all of these things from simply hearing the word "no." You have probably had similar feelings.

Yet if we remind ourselves that everything is not all about us, we will be able to step back and evaluate the response.

"Okay, big deal. Kayla said no. She said she's not able to host a show for me this summer. She's traveling a lot and her husband is having hernia repair. She said maybe in the fall. She's still my friend. She's not mad I asked. She is interested in my products. I think I'll give her a catalog and let her know how my products would turn her busy summer into more fun!"

Now, stop rolling your eyes! I'm serious! When we stop thinking about ourselves, we will be much more able to consider ways that we can help others. Perhaps your product has time-saving features. Wouldn't that be perfect for someone on the run? For someone with a recuperating husband? Think of how you can meet her needs, not the other way around.

Sadly, many of us scurry away and hide in a dark corner every time we hear the word "no." It causes us to listen far too intently to the voice of the Accuser who says, "You never should have asked! You are bothering these people! You're just trying to make money off of them!" and hundreds of others lies.

Yes, I said it. The Accuser. When you hear a voice in your head that is accusing you, it's not the sound of your own voice, or even that of your mother. It's the enemy of your soul who is whispering lies in order to keep you timid. These are lies! When someone says "no", it doesn't mean they don't like you. It often means they need more information. How can we find out what they need? By asking a simple question. "Can I answer any more questions at this time?" Frequently a "no" will turn to a "maybe" or a "yes" when you ask that. Be an overcomer! When you hear accusation or rejection, take a minute to pray and ask for wisdom and the truth. You do not need to feel downcast! You have the power and the authority to silence the accusing voices and seek the truth.

Conquering Phone Phobia

Are you afraid of the phone? I've been there. People with Phone Phobia are afraid that:

- They will be rejected
- They will be misunderstood
- They will bother someone
- They will forget what they wanted to say
- And many other fears.

(Note: if you do not have this problem, do not read these pages. I don't want to suggest fears that you don't have!)

Now, this differs from telephonophobia, the fear of the telephone. Most of us are not afraid of the actual phone itself. It's actually more a fear of making or receiving calls. In my case, it was making calls. I am fine to receive calls because I know for a fact the person wants to talk to me! If they didn't want to talk to me, they wouldn't bother calling! I am very happy to take incoming calls.

The problem is, when you are in sales, you absolutely must make outgoing calls. It's one of the major ways to build and sustain a business. The phone allows you to communicate offers, confirm attendance, answer questions and sponsor new team members. It would be very difficult to do all these things without the convenience of the phone.

"What about email?" you might be asking. Email is also a useful and valuable communication tool. It works great with those who prefer cyber-communication. You can find this out when you are first getting contact information from a customer or a prospective customer. "What's the best way to get in touch with you?" you might ask. On your contact cards, be sure to circle or star the method that works best for each person. That will give you added confidence when you see a star next to their phone number and recall that they asked you to call them.

Early on in my business days, I had a traumatic phone experience that planted fear in my heart. I was doing customer care calls…simply calling to see how they were doing, if they received my newsletter, if they needed any product and the like. I called a good customer named Heather and almost immediately she barked at me, "I can't talk to you right now, Martie!" What I heard, however, was, "I can't talk to YOU right now, Martie!" Immediately I felt both embarrassed and rejected. I assumed she meant she could make time to talk to others but definitely not me. I was humiliated. I actually burst into tears! "I thought she liked me!" I whimpered to myself.

About ten minutes later, my phone rang. I answered it, of course, since it was an incoming call. It was Heather, calling to apologize. "I am so sorry about earlier," she began.

"As soon as we started talking, I looked out the window and noticed my neighbor's house was on fire. I had to hang up to call 911." She was very nice and quite apologetic. We had a great conversation and she actually scheduled a show with me!

I learned my lesson on that call. If someone can't talk to me, it's not about me! I was so grateful that Heather called back with her explanation but many times, people don't call back to explain. That's okay! There are many situations we might be calling into. Perhaps your prospective customer has just had an argument with her teenager. Maybe she's working on her taxes; that makes everyone crabby. She could be feeling hormonal, rushing to get out of the house, or simply in a bad mood. It happens!

Create for yourself a safety net when you call. By this I mean, know that you might fall off the high wire, but you won't hit the concrete floor down below. Here are the elements of the safety net:

- Set aside quiet and uninterrupted time to talk.
- Pray before you begin!
- Ask right away, "Is this a good time?"

- Assure her the call will be brief.
- Keep it brief! Limit the conversation to one important item.
- Don't transition to gossip or small talk.
- Commit to follow up on her request, no matter what it was.

Each of these strands of the safety net are important, but none more important than prayer. If you pray before you begin, your perspective will be correct. You are calling to offer a product or service to a friend. Pray for clarity, brevity and good cheer. Acknowledge that you are an ambassador and that it's not about you. Pray for favor on your calls and on those who will be receiving them.

There is no good reason to fear the phone! It is a useful business tool and it allows you to efficiently blend your business in with all other aspects of your life. If you set aside fifteen minute increments daily to make phone calls, you will be astounded at the amount of business you have. It's just like laundry or dishes...just do it! And do not be afraid...you are not alone!

Perfect love drives out fear. 1 John 4:18

Snob Appeal

If you are a cheapskate like me, this chapter will surprise you. Many people want to be the first in town to own or use something. I call this Snob Appeal in the nicest sense of the word. There are people who want to introduce your product or service to their friends so they can get the credit. These customers appreciate name-brands, exclusive offers, and pieces signed by the artist. They are out there.

One of my dearest friends just got rid of her awesome zebra printed purse. Why? She saw too many similar purses around our town. "Many of them were rip-offs!" she told me over breakfast. Now, I was just catching on to the zebra bags and apparently they are already passé? You can see I'm not quick to grab hold of a trend. But my dear friend Jeanette is. She's the one whose ears will perk up when you say things like:

- *This is new in our town*
- *Not many people have heard of it*
- *I've never done a show in your neighborhood*
- *You can be the first to get these hostess benefits*
- *You can get products no one else has seen*
- *This is huge on the West Coast!*
- *This is really going to take off.*

These are not false statements. (The "West Coast" is just an example…but there's always a place where your product line has already been introduced!) These are facts that you are presenting. They will not appeal to everyone. The cheapskates like me will not thrill to the sound of these words. I would rather hear phrases like "special bargain" and "fifty percent off"!

There are areas in every town where Snob Appeal sells. Perhaps you need to drive out of your own neighborhood, and on the way, drive out of your own personal mind-set. This is what I had to do. I imagined that every woman in America was just like me, and would make the same exact purchasing decisions that I made. Boy, was I wrong. It was a confusing learning curve for me, which is why I want to make it a lot easier for you. Repeat after me: Not everyone is like me. And that's great!

As a cheapskate, I am much more likely to schedule a class or show. Why? Because that's usually the very best way to earn free or discounted products. Imagine my shock when I learned in my own business that some people do not care about free or discounted product! They want something different. These folks love to have the one-of-a-kind-original. They don't want to follow what everyone else is doing, they want to lead. They are a wonderful asset to your business because Snob Appeal sells. As they are sharing with their friends and neighbors what they purchased from you, they are creating a need for your product, right where they live. Have you ever noticed that once you "break in" to a neighborhood or circle of friends, you go from event to event to event among the same people? Why do you think this is? One reason is Snob Appeal. Just like the zebra purse, women want what other women have!

Other people want to be in what I call The Club. (If you don't have a "club" yet, you'll need to make one.) They want to be recognized as one of your best customers. It's important to do that! A great way is to keep track of customer purchases and do a special gift as a loyalty program. Make a big deal when your customer reaches a "loyalty level", especially with other customers around. I have known consultants who have had special events just for their very best customers. Don't keep this event a secret. Enthusiastically publicize it at your events because this will create the desire to be part of that club. Repeat hostesses are a crucial part of The Club and the better you recognize them, the more events they will host for you.

How else can you promote an exclusive club atmosphere? You are only limited by your imagination. My dear friend Gigi makes jewelry. I love the jewelry she makes but I've never seen her workshop. I suggested that she have a special event for customers who have purchased several of her pieces. We could tour her workshop (which is, in reality, a spare bedroom). And, we could make our own piece of jewelry! Voila! We would be part of an exclusive club! Be creative and think of how you could make events that recognize and celebrate loyalty.

Another friend, Rachel, organizes a scrapbook weekend and sells products there. Her husband arrives early on Saturday morning to cook breakfast for all the ladies. What a treat…especially since he is a busy local physician! Everyone who has had one of his pancakes is part of an elite society with a shared experience. I want to be part of that club! I've heard of others who take pictures of their customers as they wear or use their product. Everyone feels special having their picture taken!

As you can see, you are only limited by your imagination! Ask around…how do other consultants celebrate loyalty and sell on snob appeal? It really works!

little ideas about

dreams
&
goals

The Lord will fulfill
His purpose for me;
your love, O Lord, endures forever.

Psalm 138:8

Dreams with a deadline

As women, we are focused on the daily tasks at hand. Therefore, goal-setting can seem like one more thing on our never-ending To Do List. It's the thing that gets dropped down to the bottom of the list. There are so many daily tasks that are urgent. After all, the kids have to eat, right? And the library books returned, laundry folded, stairs swept and by golly…where has the day gone?? For many years when my five children were young, my only goal was to get an extra hour of sleep. I was simply too exhausted to dream!

Then I heard that a goal is simply a dream with a deadline. I know how to dream and I'm comfortable with a deadline. We have deadlines for everything. We need to buy presents before our child's birthday. We need to send our mom a card before Mother's Day. We need to do wash before the whole family is out of socks and underwear.

In life, if you don't meet your deadline, there is a penalty. If you don't pay your bills on time, there will be a late fee and even more interest piled on. There is always a penalty. There is also a penalty for not reaching our goals. We need to consider it every bit as important as getting those library books returned to avoid the 10 cents a day fine! We are important and worth the effort. Goals are simply dreams… with a deadline.

Dream big. What would you like to see happen in your life? What possession, material or otherwise, would you like added? For me, my dream was sending my children to Christian school. For many years, this was just a dream as I didn't do anything to advance that cause. However, when I sat down and put a date on when that needed to happen, I got serious.

I knew I wanted them in Christian school by the time they hit middle school. That gave me several years to work towards that goal. However, the bill for the school was going to be hefty. I then had to figure out the level of business I would have to attain in order to pay that bill. That gave me something concrete to work towards. I was able to break the big dream into smaller, manageable steps. It worked!

As a team leader, I learned to ask my new team members what their dreams were. (Notice I didn't ask them what their goals were. This is important because many people actually start a business without any goal other than trying it out and seeing what happens.) All women have dreams, though. One woman said, "I just want to make enough money so we can get pizza on Friday nights." I loved it. It was concrete and it represented a lot to her. She dreamed of an income that would pay for the little extras in life. Within her first month, she was buying the pizza.

What are your dreams? They must be specific. When a new team member would say, "I'd like to make some money at this," I always pressed her for more details.

"$10? $100? $1,000?" I would ask. "A week? A month? A year?"

Say she answered, "$100 profit a week." Next I'd say, "What would you spend that money on?" That's where it got fun. We dream of new clothes and summer vacations. We don't dream of paying off our Visa bills or saving for a new roof. The debt reduction and new roofs can come in time, but what are you dreaming of? Make it something you can picture. Put a photo of your dream item (or something that represents it) in your work area.

Dreams need to be specific, measurable, and reasonable. Saying, "I'd like to be a millionaire" is specific and measurable yet likely not reasonable. Dream in bite-sized pieces as you start dreaming and as you teach your team members to dream. Make your dream time specific. Say, "By the end of the year I'd like to have sponsored six new team members." Don't say, "One day I'd like to be a leader." That's not a deadline…that's just a dream!

Have a dream meeting. I once did this with my team and I was very excited about it. I put on the long, shiny dress that I wore when I promoted to Director in a direct sales company. My children asked why I was so dressed up for my meeting. My husband quipped, "Are you dreaming you still fit into that dress?" (Very funny, dear.) The kids, however, loved the idea. Kids are very familiar and comfortable with dreaming. Let them help you do it!

At the dream meeting, the table was decorated with play money. Each woman was told to take as much as she wanted. I then suggested they write what they'd spend the money on. Many dreamed of giving more money away. Awesome! I have always been challenged by people who do a "reverse tithe." They live on 10% of their income, and give 90% of it away. You can imagine that this ability did not happen overnight. It had to begin as an idea, a dream and had to be worked towards, step by step by step.

What is your dream? Write it down. A written goal is 1,000 times more likely to be achieved. Share it with those close to you. Then follow steps every day that turn your dream into a reality. And let others dream with you!

The Laundry Lesson

For many years, all I ever talked about was laundry. I'm not kidding! I gave a lot of attention to laundry. I had a laundry room in my basement. In order to enter my workshop, my customers had to walk through the laundry room. I would throw a large queen sheet over the mountain of laundry to try to hide it. That's how large the pile was. Think Mt. Everest.

Laundry consumed my thoughts. I was always behind and it bothered me. I hated all aspects of the process. I take that back. I was fine with throwing a load in the wash. That felt pretty satisfying. But then, an hour later, it needed to be dried. Then the buzzer would buzz, unheeded by me. I'd never hear the buzzer. That meant that the laundry would sit....damp, cold, wrinkled ...unfolded by me. I hated folding cold laundry but when the family ran out of clean clothes, I had no choice.

I growled about laundry, complained about laundry, and despaired over the laundry. When people asked about my business, I would say, "I do laundry full-time and my business part-time." One day, a successful business leader confronted me about my laundry obsession.

"Laundry is pretty important to you, isn't it?" Tonya asked in a direct and no-nonsense manner.

"No, it's not!" I claimed.

"Then why do you talk about it so much?" she inquired.

Good question! Why did I talk about it that much? Tonya suggested that I involve the children in doing their own laundry. Together, we schemed up a successful laundry strategy. Here are some of the tips that led to our family's laundry success.

- Keep a laundry basket in every bedroom.

- When the basket is full, the child is responsible to wash it.

- Cold water wash works for all colors.

- After the wash cycle, they put it in the dryer.

- When that's done, they are responsible to return clothes to their room.

- Because it is only their clothes, this is simple! No sorting! No orphaned socks! It's all theirs!

- All warm, dry laundry is hung on plastic hangers.

- This makes putting laundry away simple and stress-free.

- This also makes us look tidy and less wrinkled.

I became Laundry Captain instead of Laundry Queen. This meant that instead of doing all the laundry (and resenting it), I was demoted. My responsibility now became one of a "reminder" rather than a "do-er." Guess what? All of my children were fine with doing their own laundry! Our youngest child, Julia, was about 5 years old when she learned how to do laundry. She would stand on a laundry basket in order to reach our top-loading washing machine. She needed help getting her clothes in, but was thrilled to be doing a Big Kid task. I still washed the linens and the parent's clothes, but that was a drop in the bucket compared to the three loads a day I had been agonizing over! I was then free to really work my business.

There's an expression that says, "Argue for your limitations and they're yours." I realized through the Tough Love conversation with Tonya that I was using my daily tasks as an excuse. I spent more time complaining than actually doing the laundry. By verbally asserting that laundry was my most important task, I was actually holding myself back from the success that was right around the corner.

The most important thing I learned from this lesson was that I was not looking for solutions. Somehow, I was enjoying wallowing in my own limitations. Once she said, "Laundry is pretty important to you, isn't it?" the scales fell off my eyes. I could see how silly it was that I made such a big deal about the laundry. As young as they were, the kids were very capable of doing laundry! It gave them confidence and life skills that I had actually been withholding from them. I knew they would need to do their own laundry before they went off to college, but I didn't consider they could do their own laundry before they went off to kindergarten!

What is a limitation you have settled for? What excuses are you making for why you can't be more successful? What is the laundry in your life? Pray for wisdom and clarity and look for new solutions. Involve your kids. Be creative. It will make all the difference!

But I don't feel like it

What separates out the Superstars from the business Firecrackers who shine brightly at first but burn out fast? The Superstars override their emotions. You see, it's a fact of life that we're not always going to feel like doing what needs to be done. I don't take out the trash because I feel like it. I take out the trash because I like to live in a house that doesn't have overflowing trash. However, if I waited until I felt like taking out the trash, I'd live in a trash heap. Why? Because I never feel like it.

Many of us have been deluded into thinking: "If it feels right, do it." The flip side of that coin is this: "If it doesn't feel right, don't do it." But there's a problem. That's a lie! Guys, here's the fact. Work is work and it doesn't have to <u>feel</u> good to <u>be</u> good. What is the aspect of your business that you most dread? Just because you dread it, doesn't mean you don't have to do it!

Superstars override their emotions in order to get the job done. If you wait until you feel like doing your work, you may be waiting a while. In fact, you may be waiting forever. My friend Amy doesn't like to get mail out of the mailbox. She puts it off because she knows that when she gets the mail, she will need to deal with it. She'll have to sort it, pay bills, respond to invitations and the rest. To avoid the work, she just doesn't get her mail! Once her mailman asked if they had been on vacation…that's how much mail had piled up! Here's the rub. The mail still needs to be dealt with. By putting it off, it just becomes a more and more complicated process.

What are you putting off in your business because you don't feel like it? Or because you don't feel that you have the time? In my experience, many consultants who enjoy selling do not enjoy dealing with the paperwork. They put it off for months; some put it off for the whole entire year. Come tax time, they have a mess on their hands. They waited until they had "spare time" or until they "felt like dealing with it." This is not a way to run a successful business. What's the solution?

Work incrementally. Don't allow things to get away from you. For instance, it's a wonderful idea to send a brief thank you postcard to the people who have come to your show. You can get that project done at home right after the show. Or, you can wait until the end of the week and do all of your postcards at once. What you can't do is delay for a month or two. Why? One, the gesture is only effective when it's timely. Two, you will have between four and six events a month. If you write cards once a week, it will take about twenty minutes. If you wait until the end of the month, it will take several hours to complete. The reality is that you won't be able to find the hours necessary and you won't get the job done. It's a lot easier to find twenty minutes!

Parkinson's Law states that work expands to the time allotted to it. Don't allow the projects you dread to consume all of your time. If you do, you will never want to tackle them again. Discipline yourself to do the chore in a set amount of time. I actually know women who have quit their businesses because they let the paperwork get too messy and then spent far too long whipping it back into a manageable pile again. Do not let this happen to you.

Are there aspects of the business that threaten to ruin the whole experience for you? If it's honestly that bad, it's time to get some help. Maybe you don't like compiling and sending a customer newsletter, so you put it off. Instead, you might consider bartering product for secretarial help. Ask one of your trusted customers if she would be interested in some free product. Trade her product in exchange for getting your newsletter organized, copied, and mailed. Agree in advance on an hourly exchange. Since you can get your products at cost, you will be getting a bargain!

For instance, say you agree to pay Laura $5 per hour in product. She works for four hours and earns a $20 product credit with you. Your mark-up is 50%, so you are actually spending $10 to compensate her. This works well when you have customers who love your products but find that their money is tight. It's also a fantastic way to show your business to a prospective consultant. Several times after I trained a new assistant, she fell in love with the business and became a team member.

In summary, if it feels right, do it. If it doesn't feel right, still do it! Or have someone else do it. The rewards of your growing, thriving business will be more than worth it.

No Excuses

Our friend Mark gave my husband Dave great advice as he headed into a job interview. "No excuses!" Mark said sternly. "Be positive. Don't wallow in the negative." It was a good word. Dave got the job.

It's hard to live a No Excuses life. But I'm trying to. You see, we have the power to do what we want to do. If complications arise in scheduling, deadlines or life happens, we can still forge ahead. We don't need to make excuses. Even when others want us to make excuses, we can choose not to.

I've found that often we want to make excuses for why we are not succeeding. We'll say, "But I have five kids!" It's the grown-up version of "The dog ate my homework." If the dog eats your homework, you'll need to recopy it. If you want to get the job done, you will. Let nothing get in the way. Be positive!

I recently challenged myself to not make excuses, at all, for an entire year. I learned that if I wasn't going to make excuses, I would have to be much more mindful of the commitments I made. In the past I had relied on excuses to get me out of commitments that proved too difficult to honor. "I know I said I would substitute for you on Friday, Melissa, but the week got really busy for me." If you don't allow yourself this back door out of commitments, you will be careful making them. I learned how to better prioritize and say no to some projects. Both of these skills reduced my need to make excuses.

No Excuses means that you will get done what you say you will. You will not reach the day of the deadline and then start trying to justify why you couldn't do it. You will need to be both consistent and persistent to work this way. It will be well worth it in the long run. Let's get practical with what this looks like. Say your personal goal is to conduct four shows a month. That breaks down to one a week. But on your way towards this goal –surprise!— life happens.

Week 1: Hostess cancelled show
Week 2: Show is great!
Week 3: Strep throat at home; you cancel show.
Week 4: Show is great!

What do you say at the end of the month? "Oh well, I tried my best! The hostess cancelled and I had strep throat. I tried but it didn't work out. Maybe next month." This would be an extremely common response. You may even say "I'm not making excuses, I'm simply explaining. This is what really happened."

Sorry. Wrong number! You committed to four shows. Here's how the No Excuses version would play out.

Week 1: Hostess cancelled show. Reschedule it.
Week 2: Show is great!
Week 2: Have show rescheduled from Week 1.
Week 3: Strep throat at home; you reschedule show.
Week 4: Show is great!
Week 4: Have show rescheduled from Week 3.

Net result: Four shows in one month and No eExcuses. Yes, you might have to double up on some weeks in order to get the job done. But you will enjoy the success that comes when you meet your goal of four events a month. You will learn to schedule in such a way that you have a back-up plan. You may even do "back to back" shows (two in one day) as a way to stay on track.

It's your business. You can do whatever you like. Perhaps you enjoy when events cancel. It's like getting an unexpected snow day when you were in school. It's fun! But all of the cancellations will catch up with you. At the end of the year, when you go to a meeting or convention, you will be flabbergasted. The women who were sitting in your section last year have now promoted to the next level. "How did that happen?" you wonder. "Just lucky, I guess."

Then you run into these ladies at lunch and have time to catch up. You might expect that they will report a year of absolute smooth sailing. Yet when you press them, you hear that they also have lots of shows cancel and they also have sick kids. What is the difference? No Excuses. We all have life happen. Every single person who experiences success also has to blend business with the rest of her life. Perhaps her husband lost his job. Maybe she had a new baby. These are special circumstances, yes. You are your own boss and you can design a business plan that works for you and your priorities. Simply resolve that you will not fall into a pattern of making excuses for why you didn't do what you needed to do.

Once you've decided where you want to go, you make it happen. Don't make excuses to others. Don't make excuses to yourself. Yes, there will be setbacks. But expect them. As Mark advised, "Be positive! Don't wallow in the negative." Your challenge is to set a goal…then make it happen. No Excuses!

Reward Yourself

We've decided that we want to succeed and we're going to do what it takes, no matter how we feel. We're going to pick up the phone and make calls, we're going to follow up with people who have bought in the past and we're going to offer the opportunity to someone new. We may feel nervous or timid or even crabby, but we're going to do it.

I'll tell you what helps. You need to reward yourself. This needs to come from you. Be your own best friend. Treat yourself the way you wish someone else would (but doesn't.) You see, we often get stuck on the sidelines waiting for someone to cheer us on. If you are part of a team, you might want your sponsor to provide you with "atta girls." So you place a call, or send a text, or an email, detailing what you did.

Then, you sit back and wait for some sort of acknowledgement. It may come. It may not come. Either way, you are now working for the wrong reward. You are working for external affirmation. It's not a bad thing, but it's not always available. You may be disappointed. Even if you do get affirmed, it could take the wind out of your sails. Perhaps you imagine your accomplishment will earn you a cash bonus or a dinner out, and instead you get a greeting card and a potted plant. Now you don't feel affirmed, you feel disappointed. Disappointment is dangerous. You may think, "That's all I get? That wasn't worth it!" You may lose motivation and forget why you're doing what you're doing. Disappointment is the enemy of sales because it deflates you. It's hard to sell when you are deflated.

So here's what we are going to do. Agree that external affirmation is nice, but it is not necessary. We are going to affirm ourselves and we are going to start today. We know ourselves best! We know what would be a great reward. We won't have to wait to see how another responds. We won't waste any time! We can gift ourselves immediately after completing the challenge.

How do you feel rewarded? Take a few minutes and make a list. Go ahead, you can write in the book…it's yours. Write lots of things. Things that are free and things that cost money. Things that take time and things that are quick. Things that you can do right now and things that you can work towards. Be creative! What are the treats you never allow yourself? Go for it!

Maybe your list includes some of these things:

- Chocolate
- Trip to the mall
- Do my nails
- Get a pedicure
- Yummy snack
- Soak in the bubble bath
- Plant something new
- Fresh flowers in the house
- A guilt-free nap
- Phone call to old friend
- Date night with my husband
- Trip to the Bahamas

Clearly, these things range in cost and availability. They are also only a very short list of things that you may feel rewarded by. I feel rewarded by fresh popcorn. It is a very special treat for me. I love freshly popped corn, made on the stove with oil, sprinkled with salt. I love to make a fresh batch and I love to eat it all by myself. (Part of the treat is not having to share the bowl with five teenagers!) When I'm done writing this chapter, I'm going to reward myself. I'm going to make some popcorn and I'm going to eat it. I'm going to feel rewarded and I'm going to pat myself on the back. I'm going to say, "Good job, Martie. You did what you wanted to get done. You didn't stop until it was finished. Great job, in fact! Go, sit on your cozy couch and enjoy a fresh bowl of popcorn. You deserve it."

As you build a team of consultants, teach them this technique of rewarding themselves with things that they enjoy. They will be more realistic about the affirmation that you, their leader, can and should provide. They, in turn, will teach their downline how to reward themselves. It is an effective, meaningful and significant life skill.

Shampoo, Rinse, Repeat

Oh, if only life were as easy as this simple instruction. A four or five year old child can wash his own hair. Okay, not perfectly... and you'd better hope you have a bottle with No More Tears printed on it. But he can get the basic job done. By six, he can read the wisdom on the shampoo bottle. Shampoo, Rinse, Repeat. What do these instructions represent?

Repetition. Repeating the very steps that work. Here's the lesson. Life is so daily. And so is success. When you find a winning formula, repeat what you did. Repeat it over and over and over. Find what works and do it again. Shampoo, Rinse, Repeat. You've heard that there is no sense reinventing the wheel, right? That's because the wheel works, just the way it is. Consider your personal business very carefully. What are the things that work? Maybe it's a style of presentation that is unique to you. Perhaps it's a booth at a craft show. For you, success may be hosting one-on-one presentations with customers. What works best for you?

From there, it's simple. Repeat those things. Over and over and over again. It's just like washing your hair. Can you skip a step? Sure, but not very successfully. Do what works.

Shampoo.

Rinse.

Repeat.

From my experience, no matter what you are selling, you need to keep doing it. Repeat. Repeat. Repeat. When I was a sales manager, I never had someone who didn't experience at least a small measure of success. They had at least one good night. They sold a big kit. They booked another show. They came out grinning, at least one time. Firecrackers rest on that one victory.

They shine, but quickly burn out. Superstars press on. They schedule more events and perfect their techniques. In short, they repeat.

Perhaps you don't know the key success steps to repeat. Here's a simple solution for you. Find a consultant who is doing very well and learn from her. What is her formula? What are her simple steps to success? You will glean bits of knowledge from everyone you talk to. When you go to sales meetings or conventions, don't just talk to your friends or the group you came with. Walk up to people and say, "What's your best tip for success?" Write them down. Then filter through the list and resolve to add five suggestions to your weekly work plan. Don't just try these things once. Do them over and over and over again! Repeat.

Now, that's only with the techniques that work for you. Don't repeat the things that have bombed for you or for others. You've heard the definition of insanity, right? It's doing the same thing, expecting a different result. Perhaps you've invested in a booth at a craft show...and didn't sell enough product to cover your expenses. Do not repeat this experiment, hoping for a different result. That is just silly. Instead, try something new. And when you find something that is profitable for you, do it again.

This is your business. That means it has to work for you. The technique you repeat should be the one that you feel best doing. It doesn't matter what anyone else on your team is doing. Perhaps it works best when you shorten your presentation, or add humor, or add a hands-on portion to the show. Maybe nobody else in your area is doing what you are doing. That's okay! You are responsible for your own success. That includes finding out what works for you and doing it.

Shampoo, Rinse, Repeat. You'll see...the results will be beautiful!

little ideas
about
leadership

"For I know the plans I have for you,"
declares the Lord,
"plans to prosper you and not to harm you,
plans to give you hope and a future."

Jeremiah 29:11

My MBA

Ok, I'll admit it. I never did take the time to go to Harvard and get that business degree. I didn't take time for my Master's Degree....I was busy mastering skills in my own home. Somewhere between *"Everything I know I learned in kindergarten"* and *"What I didn't learn at Harvard Business School"* is what I like the call the MBA degree. Of course, we all know that the real MBA is earned on the home front; it's the Mother's Business Administration.

My MBA teaches that everyone is a contributor...whether they'd like to be or not. Therefore, if I am the CEO of a family business, the whole family is vested in it. (Again, this was not decided through a democratic vote. If I'm in and I'm your mom, then you are in.) If I have a company event here at home, the whole family pitches in. Bathrooms need to be tidied up and rooms cleaned and dusted so that we can open up our home to my business associates. No grumbling, no complaining. That's the MBA.

The MBA also states that children will allow their mom to take a business phone call without constant interruptions and distractions. I have a very sweet friend who would throw a handful of M&M's in order to get her kids to scatter when she was on an important call. I'm afraid there aren't enough M&M's in the world to keep my five children at bay. I went the stern route. This involved me making mean faces and silently counting to three on my fingers while simultaneously pointing into the other room. It works.

My MBA degree allowed me to travel for business without having petulant children at home. They might have been sad to see me go, but I never had to deal with children clinging to my legs, crying, "Don't go, Mommy!" as I endeavored to get out of town. I think this is because from very early ages they understood that our business was a family business. Sometimes their role was to stay at home and that's all there was to it.

When in pursuit of my MBA, I had many opportunities to speak. The family grew accustomed to my rehearsals. They were my audience and my judges. I would stand on the brick hearth, facing the group, and deliver my address. Comments and critiques from my stockholders would follow the speech. We're all in it together.

The MBA does require sacrifices from all family members. Often my husband would come home for his job just in time to kiss me and send me off on mine. This would mean that he would have to put some dinner together or that the kids would have cereal for dinner. Again, it was all part of the MBA.

What made getting my MBA degree both fun and a challenge was the family. I started a home-based business when my fourth child was just six weeks old. As long as the children could remember, I had a business in our home. I added our fifth child nineteen months later and never went on any type of maternity leave. By blending family and business together, I was able to do both successfully. I just kept moving forward.

The children enjoyed the MBA. They understood that benefits and privileges came from the home-based business. For instance, great snacks. They would look forward to me hosting shows and meetings in our home. They were permitted to come downstairs one time to make a little plate. All the attendees loved seeing my kids in their pajamas! After the event, they were allowed to eat all of the leftovers. This was seen as a grand perk. It got to the point that the kids were encouraging me to schedule more than one or two events a week!

We also set large and small family goals as part of the Mother's Business Administration. A small goal was money to go to a family movie which can be pretty expensive for a family of seven. Our biggest goal was to go on a Disney Cruise. As I worked my way up the career ladder, the family would celebrate by saying, "One step closer to the Disney Cruise!" When I needed to work or go out of town, I would remind the kids that I was working toward the Disney Cruise. When I promoted to

Director in my direct sales company, we went on the Disney Cruise! Every family member knew that they helped make that trip a reality.

Were there any costs to the MBA degree? Like any program, it requires an investment. The investment in this case was always time. I had to carefully and skillfully blend the time so that no member of my family was slighted. Often I was tired (lots of babies!) and yet did not allow myself a nap. My spare time was often catching up on business tasks such as phone calls or paperwork. I did wonder from time to time if this was a good example for my children. Their school work revealed that it was.

School papers carried a common theme. They would often talk about our family business or the responsibilities they had toward our success. They understood the concept of both teamwork and sacrifice. When they were running for a student office or had a book report to present, they would gather the family and deliver their speech from the hearth, just like mom. It was then that I realized that not only had I received an MBA, each of them had too!

How to be a Good Leader

We think we have to know it all in order to be effective. That's simply not true. It's not true in love. It's not true in parenting. And it's not true in leadership. It's not about where your mind is. Being a good leader is a matter of the heart.

I learned this lesson through trial and error. The Golden Rule was my guiding principle. "Treat others the way you'd like to be treated." I like a lot of affirmation. I like to be recognized in a group. I like to get fun things in the mail. I like to feel that my contributions make a difference.

This is the one instance where it was okay to make it about me. I thought of what I liked, then did it for my team members. I wanted them to feel affirmed, recognized, fun and part of a larger team. It was easy to think of ideas. I simply mused, "What would I have liked?" Then I did those things.

These ideas are perfect for celebrating the small successes along the way.

- Send an inexpensive playground ball in the mail with a note, "It's a ball having you on my team." Write directly on the ball with a Sharpie marker and yes, you can really send it!

- Hand out a sharpened #2 pencil at a unit meeting when someone shares a great tip. Say, "You are sharp!"

- Listen intently to the challenges your team members share. As soon as you get off the phone, sit down and write a note encouraging her in overcoming that specific challenge.

- Applause! In a big meeting or small, this is a universal way to say, 'Way to go!' Make it more unique by snapping your fingers instead of clapping.

- Certificates. These are easy to make up on your computer. Make them for any reason, large or small. Perhaps one says, "Most shows this month" while another says, "Overcoming fear of the phone!" Sign and date it and present it in front of an audience whenever possible.

- Special treats. At your meetings, always have special treats that you can hand out. Anything and everything looks good in a clear cellophane bag which can be inexpensively purchased online or at a party supply store. Wrap it up with curly ribbon.

- Give special treats for Most Shows, Highest Sale, Overcoming Personal Challenge, Offering the Business Opportunity and whatever else you can think of!

- Always reward the activities you want to see more of.

- Be the cheering section for each other. Don't allow your meeting times to become Pity Parties. Cheer for the good and acknowledge the challenges without getting stuck in a pit of despair. This is a skill…learn it!

- Know them well. Take the time to find out about each team member. Some leaders have a small survey for their team members to fill out. Ask things that you'd like to remember, such as husband and children's names, team member's birthday, favorite flower or candy. Only ask things that you intend to follow up on. We are loyal when we feel personally known and appreciated.

- Balloons. Is it just me or do you love balloons? This is a very easy way to say "Celebrate!" There are awesome mylar balloons available in every size and theme imaginable. When you are going to a convention or large meeting with your team, bring a balloon as a way for all to find your group. Fun, fun, fun!

- Commiserate in private. Having your own business has many challenges. Be available to listen and sympathize in private, either over coffee or over the phone. The team meeting is not the time to do this. You are her leader, yes, but you are also her friend. Listen more than you speak. Often it is enough just to know that someone listens and cares. You don't have to have all the solutions, just listen!

- Counsel blending! To be a success, you've learned how to blend your business in with the rest of your life. This is a key skill that you can pass on to your team members. They will be much happier with their business if they don't feel that it is consuming their lives.

- Model boundaries. When you send hundreds of emails to your team each week or answer their phone calls at 11 o'clock on a Sunday night, you are not being a good leader. You are modeling poor boundaries. Consolidate team news in one weekly email. Answer questions at designated times. Neither email nor call on the weekends and never on a Sunday!

- Joy in the journey. Whatever we do, do all to the glory of God. Keep the joy in the journey by not becoming overwhelmed or resentful. Remember that you are really working for an Audience of One. Pray about your business and about your team. Let them know you are open to prayer requests. Let your light shine!

Team Building for Wimps

Once you've gotten a hang of the business, and you realize it is simply "Shampoo, Rinse, Repeat," you are ready to build a team. By now you may have realized a few things. One, sponsoring a team makes the business more fun. After all, everyone wants to be a part of something special and unique. It's the #1 reason people join direct sales teams! Two, you can't do it by yourself. Whether you are selling jewelry that you designed or products from a direct sales catalog, you will find out quickly that there is more business out there than you can handle on your own. You need help. Three, in most multi-level marketing companies, sponsoring team members is the way that you will increase your personal commission as well as earn commission from your team members. It is profitable and will help you meet your goals.

You can do it! Picture that prospective team members are singing, "Take a chance on me!" Don't prejudge. Ask everyone. The simple way to gain confidence in team-building is to begin by asking your most impassioned customers if they'd consider the business. They are the ones who buy a lot of product. They arrange a lot of shows for you. They tell all of their friends about your offerings and they squeal with excitement when new products are available. They are your best customers, and they will be your best new team members. That is, if you share the opportunity with them.

Who offered the chance to you? Aren't you glad they did? Or perhaps you are the inventor, the artist, the only who is currently selling your product. If so, you are the First Generation in your sales line. Everyone that you come into contact with either knows you directly or knows of you through a friend. As word spreads, though, this will no longer be the case. You'll start selling to the friend-of-a-friend-of-a-friend-of-a-friend.

Everyone deserves to have a First Generation consultant. This is someone who is in their circle, in their neighborhood, or in their part of town. This makes order filling simple and creates loyalty. It also makes it less likely that your customer's eyes will wander to another consultant or another product line altogether. Simply stated, our job is to make it easier to buy than to not buy. Therefore, think of it as good customer service when you launch new team members. Freely give referrals from your customer base to the consultants you are sponsoring.

Here's how I did it. Imagine Sheila has a show for me. She brings 12 friends. 8 of the 12 become great customers. Sheila has a second show. 6 more of her friends start buying. I now have 14 good customers that came through Sheila. But that's not all. Several of Sheila's friends have scheduled their own events. This is a perfect time to offer the business opportunity to Sheila. Why?

She will start with scheduled events which will help her hit the ground running. Her friends will be even more likely to schedule and buy from her than you. Her friends have not yet had a chance to become attached to you, your inventory or your way of doing business. They will be loyal to Sheila and excited to help her get her business up and running. Take a chance on Sheila by offering her the opportunity to become a member of your team. But make sure that Sheila understands that if she does not accept the invitation, you will be asking her friends next!

Fear is the biggest obstacle to team building. Fear whispers in your ear that you won't be a good sponsor, that you won't know how to answer questions, or that it will take up too much of your time. These are not true! In fact, you will be a good sponsor because you'll be honest, encouraging and engaged. That's all it takes! You'll honestly answer questions that come up but you will also be forthright to admit when you don't know the answer to a question. Promise you will find out and get back to her in a reasonable amount of time. Sponsoring is the single best use of your time. It's the gift that keeps on giving.

You've already figured out that you are only one woman. Say you can devote one night a week to a show. If you sponsor one team member and she follows your lead of one event a week, that's your team out two nights a week. You've doubled the exposure through one team member. Do the math! The bigger the team, the bigger your overall success!

Are you afraid you won't be a good leader? This is similar to not wanting to have a baby because you don't know how to deal with <u>teenagers</u>. Did you know everything about parenting before you began your family? Probably not! I'm sure you read books, got advice and learned as you went along. This is the same for team building. Your team will love you! As long as you are honest, true and enthusiastic, they will easily forgive any gaffes or missteps.

As I reflect back on my career, my team times were the highlight. I loved being part of a team, sort of like a sorority but with a commission check. I loved treating others the way I'd like to be treated. I decorated their hotel room doors at conventions, made crowns when they promoted, and sent cute notes and things in the mail. It was a lot of fun. We grew together and encouraged one another. I did not set out to build a large team, but I quickly realized that my team made every part of my business more enjoyable. I just kept sharing as I went along the way and great people accepted the opportunity and came along for the ride. It was wonderful and we made memories I will never forget!

Thanks, Shining Stars. I love you guys!

Just Keep Swimmin'!

In the kid's movie Finding Nemo, Dory says to Marlin, "Just keep swimmin', swimmin', swimmin'....." In other words, the only way to make progress is to keep moving! This is also great advice for having your own business. The way to success is to keep swimin', er, asking. Just keep askin', askin', askin'! This is not being a nag. It's being a success! You see, most people do not agree to anything on the very first invite. I once read that 80% of people respond after having heard the offer four or more times. 80%! The vast majority of people need to be asked more than once. Think about it. Do you respond the first time you are asked? Likely not! Most of us are part of that 80% and we need frequent reminders!

I was recently invited to a party-plan show at a friend's house. She sent me a postcard in the mail. This promptly got lost in the big mail basket in our house. I am not one of those people who look at mail once, deal with it and then file it. I'm part of the Stacker Society. You know, I stack things up. Often when I go through the basket, response dates have already come and gone. This causes me to miss lots of events (and also pay late fees on my bills.) I know I'm not the only one.

What Melanie did next was unusual. She sent an evite (email invitation) to follow up on her paper invitation. This was brilliant. She effectively re-invited all of her postcard guests and also added names to the guest list. I was very impressed by the evite for several reasons. It was very cheery. The language was fun and I didn't feel pressured in any way. The event was going to be held on May 5th which is Cinco de Mayo. She brightly offered "margaritas for my senoritas." I was sold! I loved the idea that I was one of Melanie's senoritas! The follow-up, the cheery language, the sense of being one of the chosen invitees....all of these made me much more likely to respond in the affirmative.

Guess what happened? I couldn't go. I looked at my calendar and it wasn't a great day for the family. But now, thanks to my two invitations and the good cheer, I took the time to respond to her e-invitation. The evite made it easy for me to respond, thanking her for the invitation and offering my regrets. It was, for me, much, much easier and faster than calling Melanie with my regrets. I have to confess, I've been invited to many events over the years and shamefully, I have often been the friend who doesn't even respond. Even after being in direct sales, and knowing what bad etiquette it is to not respond, I still do it. Why? Because I don't want to get caught in a lengthy conversation with the hostess. And because I don't want to be made to feel guilty in any way. Therefore, I understand when people don't respond. It's our job to make it easy for them to RSVP.

What is the lesson? Just keep invitin', invitin', invitin'! There are several different ways that you can contact someone with an opportunity. You can:

- *Invite in person*
- *Call on the phone*
- *Mail*
- *Email*

I recommend doing all of the above. Some people are happy to get a phone call. Others love mail! Some are most efficient when in front of their calendar and their computer. They will appreciate the email. How do you know what people will best respond to? You won't know! That is why you need to keep up a steady rotation of all the methods of asking. It's just like the different learning styles. You've heard that some people learn best by reading, others by listening, still others by doing. These are all effective ways to learn. Similarly, some will respond to one method of asking, others will respond to another. No method is superior. Different methods work for different people.

We assume that the method that works best for us is the best method. This is not the case. We also give up far too easily. We think if we've mentioned our business once or twice and our friend has not shown interest, she will never be interested. This could not be farther from the truth. In this busy and hectic world, it's likely that the first two mentions went in one ear and out the other. You don't want to badger her. (Please don't badger her!) But you do want your friend to be involved. How can you "keep swimmin" in that situation?

If you have a wearable product, wear it! If you have a product that's edible, bring it to events when you are together. Make it part of who you are. Your third, fourth and fifth invitations for your friend to get involved can be nearly unspoken. I guarantee when you open your mouth and ask her again, she will be ready to engage in a conversation. "What are you doing, again?" she may ask. Don't feel frustrated, knowing you've already told her. Celebrate that now she is ready to listen and respond. Hurray!

It's been said that 80% of people respond to the fourth or fifth invitation. But guess what? 20% of salespeople give up after the second or third invitation. Who gets the most business, then? The person who keeps asking! Just keep swimmin', guys. You'll be glad you did!

Run to the Problem

Is resolving conflict one of your favorite things to do? I didn't think so. Yet, it is so important. I rarely meet a woman who says that she likes confrontation. Most of us prefer that everyone get along. At least, we say that. Sadly, feelings are hurt and things are said that cause misunderstandings. If these issues are not addressed, they will grow and damage our business. The best advice I ever heard was "Run to the problem."

What does this mean? It means that when there is a problem, run to it and solve it. Do not run away from it! Do not stick your head in the sand and hope it will go away. It will not go away. It will either be purposefully resolved or it will grow into a bigger problem. Either way, you will have to deal with it eventually. Why not today?

Say one of your customers is dissatisfied with the service she's gotten from you. Perhaps she's left you a phone message or two and you've overlooked them. (I'm sure you had reason to do this, but now it's been done and needs to be undone.) Customer X, let's call her Sally, is now complaining about you to Customer Y. Customer Y, Francine, calls to tell you what Sally is saying. What do you do?

- Complain about Sally to Francine?
- Make excuses to Francine?
- Get defensive?
- Cross Sally off your customer list?

None of these are the correct response. Instead, you'll need to take a minute, prepare your heart, and eat a piece of humble pie. Thank Francine for caring enough about you and your business to call and tell you. Then immediately set out to make it right with Sally. Do not delay! Why? Because now Francine will tell Sally that she's spoken to you. If you put off your apology for a week or gasp, a month, Sally has all the more reason to be frustrated with you! Run to the problem!

Say a prayer for the right words and right heart, then call Sally immediately. Apologize right away for not getting back to her sooner. Ask what you can do to help her. Listen to every word she says. Take notes so you are sure you understand her issue. Resist the urge to argue or defend. Simply listen. Listen, listen, listen.

When Sally is done speaking, say, "I hear what you are saying." Restate her explanation so it is clear you do understand. Rephrase what she shared like this: "You are frustrated because your product arrived damaged and you tried to let me know about it. You left me two messages and I didn't call you back. Is that right?" When she agrees, apologize again. Do not make excuses! Offer to make it right. If it's a problem with a product, replace it immediately. If it's an issue with an event, ask her how you can make it up to her. Gifts are always a great way to make everyone feel better. Perhaps you have a retired hostess gift that you can give to Sally along with her new order.

This does not need to be a long call. Thank her again for the time. Then follow up this conversation with a short note to both Sally and Francine. Short and sweet. Use your cute note cards and thank each again for the business and the conversations. Now, doesn't that feel better?

Sometimes hurt feelings arise among your team members. Set the standard in your team that you will not be gossiping or backbiting. That sounds so obvious but it's been my observation that gossipy teams have gossipy team leaders. This is not a girls club but a business. We need to respect and honor each other. When there is an issue between two team members, speak to each individually. Practice active listening where you listen then rephrase what they've shared. Allow them to air their feelings without malice towards another. Then set up a time that you can get together and reconcile the differences.

Often conflicts arise over customers. Perhaps Mary is upset that her neighbor is now buying from Sue rather than from Mary. The customer is always right. Mary's neighbor has the prerogative to buy from whomever she chooses. However, Sue must not actively recruit Mary's customers. Mary is angry because she feels that is just what Sue has done. It's appropriate that both Mary and Sue state their case, but that they both understand that the customer chooses her own consultant. The customer is always right. There are plenty more prospective customers and it's a waste of time, effort and teamwork to squabble over one or two.

Conflicts of any type among your team members will hurt your business in the long run. An amazing amount of time can be spent nursing hurt feelings. Issues easily get blown out of proportion. You will be expected to take sides but resist the urge. Be neutral and fair. Hear everyone out. Be a peacemaker! All you will feel is good.

Seek peace and pursue it. Psalm 34:14

The Theme Team

Have you noticed that as grown-ups, our opportunities to be silly and dress up are very limited? Our dressing up is along the lines of getting a new dress for Easter or our niece's wedding. Life plods along and we become the women we said we wouldn't be. We don't want to get our hair wet at the pool, we don't put on a costume for any reason, and in short, we get all serious and adult.

Do you miss it? Miss the fun? Being silly and being with others who are doing the same? It's astounding how much more fun we can be having. So, have a theme event. Use any excuse. One of my team members, Michele, had a Hawaiian style party to promote her business. She wore a grass skirt and a bikini top. (For the sake of modesty, and because it was winter, she wore her silver bikini on top of a white t-shirt.) Her friends came, also in costume, but they all seemed stunned by her attire. One finally got up the nerve and asked, "Michele, why are you wearing a bra on top of your shirt?" They couldn't tell it was a bikini or even Hawaiian attire. Everyone had a good laugh and I still giggle when I remember it.

Have fun! Once I hosted an event where everyone was encouraged to bring their high school yearbook along. It was hilarious reading the captions and seeing the pictures. Another time we all brought our wedding pictures. What a great way to reminisce and get to know others. One lady even brought the little crown that she wore to her wedding. For snack I served a white cake, of course, and little mints. It was a blast.

Your team can have its own mascot and team name. I really encourage this. Is it strictly necessary? Of course not. Will it add to the fun and adventure? Definitely! I have always loved stars so my team was, of course, The Shining Stars. JoAnna chose the bumblebee as her mascot and her team was the Bee-lievers. Sondra chose angels. Amy chose anchors and the tagline "Christ is the anchor of family and business."

Once you have a team name and mascot, it's easy to promote team spirit. I loved the star theme because it's very easy to find cards, wrapping paper and small gift items with the star theme. I always encouraged my leaders to pick a theme that they already loved. Hearts, butterflies, firecrackers. It really doesn't matter, as long as it's something you love. A team name helps the team to work cohesively instead of as individuals. Themes add fun to your team meetings and newsletter. It also helps to take the focus off the leader and onto the team members. The Shining Stars is a lot more inclusive and descriptive than "Martie's team." It's not about me, after all!

Some might say that this is a business, not a girls club. I agree…and I disagree. It's a business in how we conduct ourselves. We need to be honest, sincere, committed and responsible. It's a girls club in that we primarily sponsor other women in joining our business. We join together with shared dreams and goals. We like to laugh and be frivolous. Why not have some fun with it?

Tiaras are a hit among women of any age. Why not buy an inexpensive tiara at your local dollar store? Let the top performer wear it at each meeting. For promotions to the next level, I always made a tiara out of star garlands with hanging curly ribbon. (I am always stocked up on star garland and curling ribbon of all colors!) The honoree got to wear her crown during the meeting and take it home with her. It was always met with glee by the woman who always knew she was a princess and was just waiting to be discovered! What a simple way to show your team member how honored and valued she is. It cost about fifty cents to make but was literally priceless! Go ahead, celebrate her inner royalty.

For inspiration on naming your team or thinking of fun theme events, you don't need to look farther than your local party supply store. You'll get lots of ideas there. Order a copy of the Oriental Trading Company catalog and let your imagination run wild. It's a great idea to choose a color theme for your team, just like the sports teams do. Like the teams, you will build recognition and team loyalty through the simple use of colors. Unlike the teams, you can go wild! Maybe your favorite colors are pink and green. Go for it! Whenever you see pink and green items, you can pick them up and add them to your supplies for team and customer events. It's a fast, simple and effective way to create team loyalty.

Once, when invited to wear the color blue to a leadership event, our team went dressed as the Blues Brothers. We got our pictures taken with all the corporate executives and made it into the company magazine. What a great memory. Be creative. Have fun and be inspired by things around you! Think of the symbols that mean a lot to you and build from there. Awesome teams have started with inspiration like Dorothy's ruby slippers or Tinkerbell's wings. You are never too mature or too successful to laugh until your belly hurts and lead others to do the same!

little ideas
about
what
really
matters

*Everyone who calls
on the name of the Lord
will be saved.*

Acts 2:21

Take a Chance

What does that phrase make you think of? Exciting opportunities? Or fear and rejection? I asked a bunch of middle school students what this phrase meant to them. I was substitute teaching at my children's school one day and this concept was on my mind. I wrote "Take a Chance" on the board and listened to what they said. This is how the kids responded:

- Try
- Live life on the edge
- Take risks
- Speed
- Get over fears
- Forgive
- Try
- Sky diving
- Guess
- Don't leave things blank
- Try something new
- Be bold
- Gamble
- Try
- Risk
- Trial
- Brave
- Don't judge

Clearly, they get it. Take a chance is simply an attitude of trying. I was astounded at how many times they answered, "Try." Simply try. Guess if you have to, but try! Fascinated at their bravery, I asked them, "If you're not 100% successful 100% of the time, are you a failure?"

Of course the answer is "No!" Kids get it. I think that part of the problem with adults is that we get stuck in a place of fear. Even the phrase "Take a Chance" seemed laced with fear and risk for me. Risk of failure, risk of rejection. Those are uncomfortable things that we'd rather not experience. To protect ourselves, we make excuses and we simply don't put ourselves out there. But the kids have something here. When asked, "Is this a negative or a positive phase?" most kids said, "It's positive." We need to think like kids!

One skinny 7th grader even said, "It depends on how you look at life, as the glass half empty or half full." In our youth, we are used to taking chances. You ride your bike down the biggest hill in the neighborhood simply because you want to. You don't think, "What if I fall? What if I break my bike? What if I break my head?" These are adult concerns. You see the hill and you ride down it. You take a chance. Or, you ask your crush to the prom. You screw up your nerve and you just ask. Maybe the answer is yes, sometimes, heartbreakingly, it's no. But you try!

If you are not trying, you are not trusting. Trust acknowledges that we are not in control of every situation and yet we make our peace with that. We can't see the future, but we can trust that it will be okay. Trust and faith are the antidotes to fear.

Trust in the LORD with all your heart and lean not on your own understanding; in all your ways acknowledge him, and he will make your paths straight.

Proverbs 3:5-7

How to make my Lord your Lord

I grew up going to church. We went almost every Sunday. This was a real drag for me because there were no cute boys in our church. Sadly, that is what I remember most. Confirmation class was practically torture because of the no cute boy factor. I tried to talk myself into having a crush on the one 8th grade boy in that class, but to no avail. I grew up in church, but I wasn't really there, if you know what I mean.

College was a four-year party. Career was when I started to pay attention to life around me. I was sad, confused and tired. "If this is all there is to life, I'm not sure I want to stick around." I remember often having that thought. I would drive down the beautiful towns on the Main Line outside of Philadelphia, and look at all the lovely stone churches. I thought there might be something for me within their walls, but I was too intimidated to go see for myself.

So I started researching other world philosophies which might add significance to my lonely life. New Age was interesting with its emphasis on self. But the crystals just seemed ridiculous to me and I knew that it wasn't the truth. Co-workers and dear friends were Jewish. That fascinated me. I loved the holy days and knew as much about them as some of my friends. The process to convert was arduous, though, and I knew from the outset that I wasn't really committed…I just wanted to be part of the club.

At the end of 1989, something wacky happened. I met a cute man on a plane. We talked for the entire five hour flight. Although he lived in a different state, he offered to drive up and take me out to lunch sometime. I was skeptical but the conversation had been great. I said yes and we exchanged phone numbers on the back of our boarding passes. His name was Dave.

Dave did indeed call and drive from Annapolis to Philadelphia to take me to lunch. The lunch turned to dinner and the conversation deepened. Over dinner he started to talk about his faith in Jesus Christ. I felt very uncomfortable. In our church growing up, we talked about God but not about Christ. We certainly didn't speak of Christ as if He was someone we knew, who was in the same restaurant, and even in the same conversation. I felt sad because I thought this guy Dave was pretty cool but now he turned out to be some type of Jesus Freak. But something in me agreed to another date. It was only a number of weeks before we both felt that we were falling in love. Dave then gave me an unusual gift, at least I thought it was odd. He gave me my first Bible.

"Start at the Gospels…Matthew, Mark, Luke and John," he advised.

"You can't start a book in the middle!" I scolded.

"It's actually the beginning of the second section," Dave assured me. "It's allowed."

It was a crazy ride. Some of the stories seemed a bit familiar to me, from my days in Sunday school, but most of it seemed very new. I remember thinking, "This Jesus is cool!" He was not at all what I had expected. He was full of love and compassion and peace. He didn't rush and He didn't judge. He listened and He calmed the storm. I started to fall in love…this time with this Jesus that Dave knew and loved. Yet something was holding me back. Those college years and all the choices that I had made, well, it didn't seem like such a party anymore. I had deep regrets. I imagined that those old choices would keep me from a new way. My deepest desire was that I could push a "re-do" button and start a whole new life. I wished that I could be new but I remembered with shame and disgust some of my earlier actions. If I felt that way, what would a holy God think of what I had done? I felt stuck.

Dave and his whole family prayed. It wasn't that they wanted me to join their club. It was that they wanted me to have the freedom they experienced. Dave invited me to a Christian seminar and while some of it was poignant, much of it was boring. Attending after a long day at work, I often dozed off. Then, one night, I heard some things that cut through my fatigue and my anxiety.

- *"Your past transgressions are as far as the East is from the West."*

- *"You can be born again."*

- *"In Christ you are a new creation...the old is gone, the new has come."*

- *"Christ died once for all."*

- *"You are forgiven."*

These promises from the Bible were exactly what I had hoped and dreamed of. I could be new. I would be accepted. I could press the re-do button and enter into a new life with Christ. His sacrifice was enough...I just needed to believe and receive. I wasn't alone! "All have sinned and fall short of the glory of God." His death cancelled out my sin forever. I raised my hand, like a little kid at school, and received. It was that easy. It was that complicated.

Since then, I've grown in the knowledge of Christ and love Him, the lover of my soul. I find Him everywhere I go...in nature, in His Word, in the kids. I want to share the joy and freedom that I found with everyone I meet. It's my very favorite thing to talk about. I'd love to share with you. Oh yes, and I'm sure you figured it out....Dave and I got married ten months after we met, courtesy of U.S. Air and the eternal God who has a great sense of humor.

Confessions of a Former Know-It-All

I'm scared of people who know it all. I know a few of them. I recognize the species. Because, well, I used to be one. I knew it all. At least, I thought I did. When I was younger, hoooo baby, you could not tell me anything. I knew it all. I look back now and blush. If I had addresses, I'd send out lots of sympathy cards. I'd write to everyone who used to work with me, for one. I'd say....

Sorry you had to work with me in the 80's. I know I was really obnoxious. Thanks for not throwing me out the window of our high story office building. Blessings! Martie

I bet some people are still mad. Like one lady chased me into the bathroom once and yelled at me through the stall. She told me I was young and I didn't know what I was saying. I sat on the toilet and thought about how wrong she was. Sorry, Kate. To Kate, I should send flowers.

My gosh, the moral fiber I imagined that I had! The stand that I took on so many issues! Ok, it's a tiny bit cute now, to remember how very brilliant I felt when I argued with adults. I felt powerful! I felt right! I could not be dissuaded! On the other hand, now that I have teenagers and have those arguments in reverse, it's not all that cute. It's annoying.

When did I figure out that I didn't know it all? I guess it started when I met the Lord. You see, the very first thing I learned about God was this. *"He removes our past transgressions as far as the East is from the West."* (Psalm 103:12, paraphrase mine.)

This was both reassuring and humiliating. It was reassuring because I was dragging a lot of baggage around with me. I wasn't quite sure how I'd ever be free of it. It was great to know that it could be sent through some heavenly FedEx to the other end of the earth. It was humiliating because if God was going to perform that service for me, gosh, it meant He knew what all the transgressions were. He knew it all. It wasn't me who knew it all, it was God. Gosh, that was painful….but freeing at the same time.

Well, the more I grow in the Lord, the more I realize that I don't know it all. I hardly know anything. But I'm psyched because God really does know everything. And He still loves us. He knows what happened in the past. He knows what will happen in the future. He even knows every word we're going to say, before we say it.

(When I found that Scripture, I was fascinated! Every word? Before we say it??? To test this out, I shouted out a swear word, a really bad one, really fast. And I felt the Lord kind of smirking, with a knowing grin on His face. *"I knew you were going to say that,"* He said.)

You can't get away from the Lord. And that's a great thing.

So now I know that I don't know much. And I'm pretty relaxed about it. See, the view is nicer from the "Don't Know It All" side of the fence. You don't have to always be arguing. You don't have to think how stupid everyone else is all the time. You can just hang out, and love people.

So now when I meet a Know-It-All, I just smile. And throw up a silent prayer that the Lord will grab hold of them, and save them from themselves, like He did with me. I'm really grateful. I don't know much…but I do know Him.

Turns out, that's All.

It's Not About Me

There are two types of vanity. One is thinking very highly of
yourself. The other is thinking you are nothing. Both of these
are forms of pride. Whether you suffer from one or the other,
you need to repeat these words, "It's not about me!" You are
here by order of the King on an important assignment to Planet
Earth. You have been gifted and skilled. You are called to help
and bless others. That's what it's about.

The Bible says that we should not think of ourselves more highly
than we ought, but with sober (realistic) judgment. The
converse, of course, is that we should not think of ourselves as
lower or less than we really are. Low self esteem is pride that
goes underground. It still shows that you think it's all about
you...just in a negative, not positive light. We can only repair
our self-esteem by taking "self" out of the mix. Instead, we need
to have God-esteem. This is what I've learned....

It's about Him, not me. He made me. He called me out of
darkness. He calls me his beloved. My own emotions may lie to
me. I know they do. I have never been invited to speak
somewhere without getting absolute flop sweats the day of the
presentation. I feel in my heart, "They don't really want me
here. This is a big mistake." Those sentiments feel very, very
real. (I've had to pray in earnest to make myself get out of my
car and walk into a meeting that I've been invited to! Doesn't
that sound ridiculous?) It <u>feels</u> real, but it's <u>not real</u>.

Yet, I can't persuade myself by using my own wisdom and
counsel. It just doesn't work that way. I have to take it to a
higher authority. I know how I feel...but what is the truth?
There is Truth with a capital T. It is not what the world says. It
is not what Glamour magazine says. It is not what your high
school coach says. It is not what your boss, your mother or your
husband says about you.

The absolute Truth is found in God's word. The Truth is that God calls me His workmanship, His poem. He promises to love me with an everlasting love. He assures me that He will never leave me or forsake me. He is enthralled by my beauty! He is my Lord! That is the truth. That is God-esteem.

The secret, then, is to not evaluate yourself by the mirror or by comparing yourself with others. (What they are wearing? Saying? Thinking? Doing?) You do have an audience…but it's not the one you think you have. You have an Audience of One. Jesus Christ is the One. He is the Way. He is the Truth. He is the Life. He is the Word, the living Word. Who does the Word say I am?

Who Am I in Christ?

I Am:

A Child of God. *1 John 3:10*
Above and not beneath. *Deuteronomy 28:13*
The apple of my Father's eye. *Psalm 17:8*
The aroma of Christ. *2 Corinthians 2:15*
Called by God. *Hebrews 5:4*
Chosen by God. *1 Thessalonians 1:4*
Christ's ambassador. *2 Corinthians 5:20*
Comforted by God. *2 Corinthians 1:4*
Complete in Christ. *1 John 2:5*
Crucified with Christ. *Galatians 2:20*
Forgiven of all my sin. *Matthew 26:28*
God's field and God's building. *1 Corinthians 3:9*
His faithful follower. *Revelation 17:14*
Light of the world. *Matthew 5:14*
Loved by God. *Romans 1:7*
Salt of the Earth. *Matthew 5:13*
Set free. *John 8:6*
Strong in Christ. *1 Peter 5:10*
Temple of the Holy Spirit. *1 Corinthians 6:19*

These are the promises for believers in Jesus Christ. There are many, many more. Make the Truth your filter for how you act and how you feel. Surround yourself with the Word and do not rely on your emotions or what others say. Build your house…and your business…on the rock, Jesus Christ.

This list comes from my friend Jenn Fountain. She has designed these affirmations into beautiful magnets that you can put on your fridge. They are a great way to remind yourself every day of the truth of who you are in Christ. They are an awesome way to teach your children the Truth, too.

To order sets of these affirmations, log on to www.jennfountain.com.

About the author

Martie Smith Byrd is an encourager. She loves to speak to groups large and small. She shares with humor and spice on a variety of topics ranging from parenting, faith, business and life. She was an award-winning advertising copywriter in Philadelphia until she began her family. She had five children in six years while maintaining a highly successful home-based business. Martie retired as a Director with a vibrant team to focus on writing and speaking. She is a follower of Christ and loves to let His light shine wherever she goes!

Martie grew up in Simsbury, Connecticut. She and her husband, Dave, met on a plane in Texas. They have five gorgeous and talented children: Alex, Daniel, Trevor, Caroline and Julia. They live in beautiful Roanoke, Virginia, the Star City of the South.

Martie is a monthly columnist in the Southwest Virginia regional magazine, Bella. Her column, "Welcome to my World," is about her household of teens. She is the author of two books: *Little Ideas, Big Results* and *The Kids Drank Pickle Juice*. For copies, please contact the author directly. There is a wonderful quantity discount!

Martie would love to come speak to your group or organization. To contact her with a speaking request, please email martiebyrd@yahoo.com. To read more encouragement, log on to www.martiebyrd.com.

Commit to the Lord whatever you do, and your plans will succeed.

Proverbs 16:3

Martie and the Laundry Team

Trevor, Julia, Alex, Caroline and Daniel

Photo by Dave "Happy Daddy" Byrd

Mother's Day 2009

The Kids Drank Pickle Juice

Martie Byrd

I live at Hormone Central. I'm a 40ish mom and hormones are messing me up. You know what I'm talking about. Acne and unwanted hair and insane mood swings and chocolate cravings and tears. And that's just Monday. But it's not just my hormones. Add to the mix our 3 teenaged sons. Testosterone drips from the walls in our house. That's some powerful stuff, testosterone. Sure it's cool that they can leap tall mountains in a single bound. My oldest does chin ups from the door jams and admires his muscles when he thinks we're not watching. He's 16…enough said. Next in line are identical twins who are 14. They know everything and come in stereo. Think that's enough hormones for one house? NAH! Next we have a few girls. We have a pre-teen (11) and tweenaged girl (age 9). Who designates these stages, I don't know. But my 11-year-old puts her hands on her newly formed hips and assures me that she is a pre-teen. I know not to argue. And my baby, aged 9, acts like Hannah Montana and has more earrings than I do. Welcome to my world.

How did I get into this mess? By having 5 kids in 6 years. And yes, we did it on purpose. We wanted a large family and by golly, that's what we got. We had our first 3 boys in 18 months. That was the stage when I was nearly bald. I imagined that I looked like Demi Moore in *Ghost*. With 3 babies, I didn't have time for a shower, never mind a hairstyle. My husband said, "It takes a strong man to be married to a woman with no hair." Who asked him, anyway?

Dave asked on our first date how many kids I wanted to have. Not if I wanted kids…how many. I didn't realize that he was looking for a breeder to carry on the Byrd traits. But then child after child came out as mini-Dave's. They all arrived with the same checklist. Blonde hair? Check. Pointy chin? Check. Porcelain skin? Check. I was the human incubator, turned laundress, chief cook and slave. Ah, the joys of motherhood.

Back then, when Dave probed about how many of his children I'd like to have, I answered, "As many as we could emotionally and financially handle." Now we laugh and say, "And then we had four more." See, now that we have a houseful of teens, we realize that we can't handle it. But it's too late. You can't put them back. They're too big. And most of them could carry me around, rather than the other way around...

I have finally reached the age when I realize I don't know it all and guess what? Now my kids do. They know everything and I don't. Stupid, stupid, stupid Mom. One of my 14-year olds constantly argues. He argued with me about the day of his birth. He remembers it better than I do. He actually said that. About the day he was BORN. You see what I am dealing with?

Laptop at the ready, I now have this cool chance to set the record straight. I'll write all about my family and you, loyal readers, can take my side. Someone has to take my side. You see, when I think of life at home with all these kids/hormones/opinions, one phrase comes to mind.

The Lunatics Have Taken Over the Asylum.

Thanks to _my_ hormones, I'm just about at that age when I can't remember a single thing. But here's the problem. The lunatics, er, kids in my house, have figured that out. They use my absent-mindedness against me. They know it all…and remember everything. My eldest just told me this week, "You stink at math and you have a bad memory." (Remember when they used to think that Mommy hung the moon and stars?) He's the first one to get out of trouble by asserting, "But I TOLD you where I was going."

Did he tell me? I can't remember. Their hormones give them courage. My hormones give me confusion. See how it's toxic? And a whole lot of fun

Shine Like Stars

Shine like stars
In the universe
As you hold out
The word of life.

Philippians 2:15-16

A ministry of encouragement for women.

www.martiebyrd.com
(540) 563-9898
martiebyrd@yahoo.com

CANDID REVIEWS

Martie has a lively and humorous style that is very engaging. She is practical in her approach to a topic - she shares principles and practices in a way that can be easily grasped and applied by her listeners. She speaks from personal experience, giving her credibility with her audience.

Martie is REAL.

Barbara McCandless, Norfolk, VA

"Martie's words and passion for the Lord blessed the women of our church in so many ways. Though we were only with her for a weekend, the impact has been far reaching! We could feel and see her relationship with Jesus Christ in every word, every prayer and every funny moment of the weekend. Martie, thank you for sharing your experiences and your heart with us! It was an incredibly moving and inspirational weekend, a retreat that changed lives and hearts!"

Kris Kuester, New Hanover Presbyterian Church,
Mechanicsburg, VA

"Martie, I wanted you to know how thankful I am for your leadership, talent and enthusiasm that transformed our women's retreat into a weekend of godly renewal! You have certainly found your calling. May God continue to bless you and your family to permit you to serve Him in such amazing ways!"

Cheryl Lafferty, Mt. Pisgah United Methodist Church,
Midlothian, VA

www.ingramcontent.com/pod-product-compliance
Lightning Source LLC
Chambersburg PA
CBHW031952190326
41519CB00007B/767